# My Best Friend A to Z

## *Fill In The Blank Gift Book*

Published by K. Francklin

Cover Image: Produced by K. Francklin

© Copyright 2015

ISBN-13: 978-1517788391

ISBN-10: 1517788390

To _____

You're My Best Friend
Because…

From _____

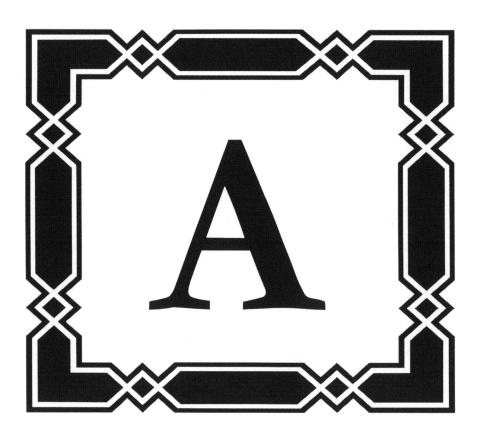

# You are...

A_____

# You are...

# B_____

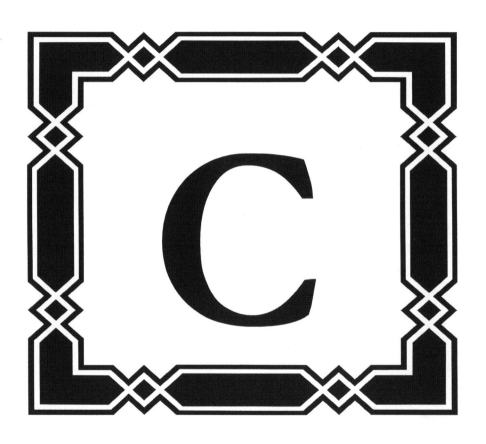

# You are...

C_____

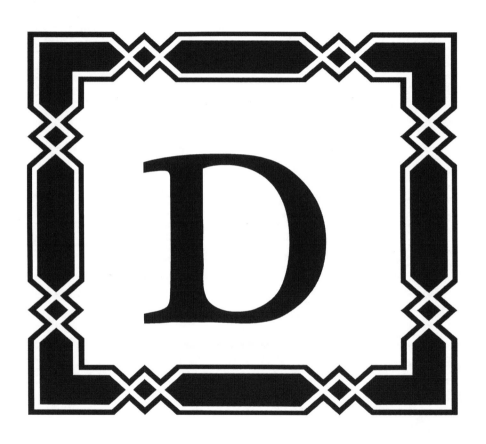

# You are...

# D_____

You are...

E_____

# You are...

F_____

# You are...

# G_____

# You are...

## H_____

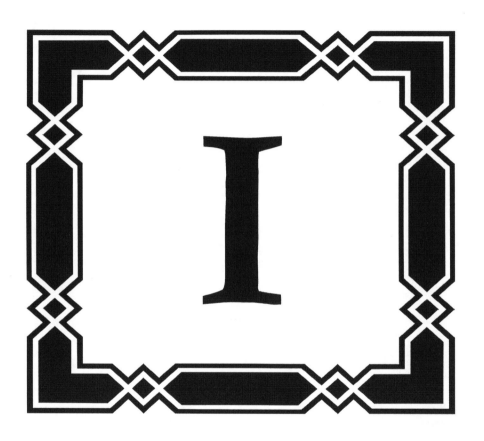

# You are...

I_____

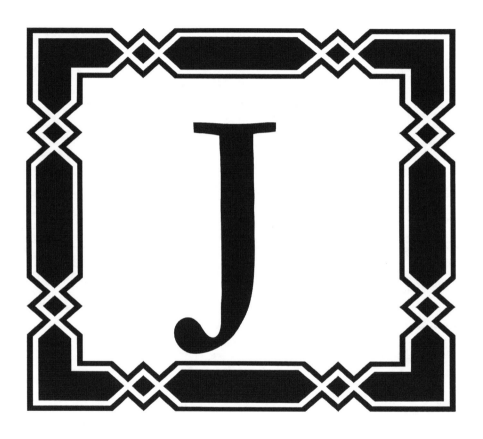

# You are...

J_____

# You are...

K_____

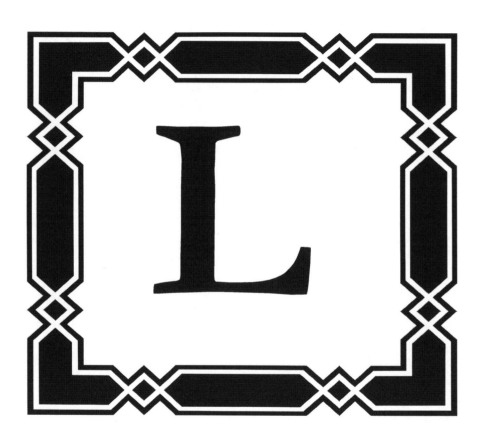

# You are...

# L_____

You are...

M_____

# You are...

N<u>_____</u>

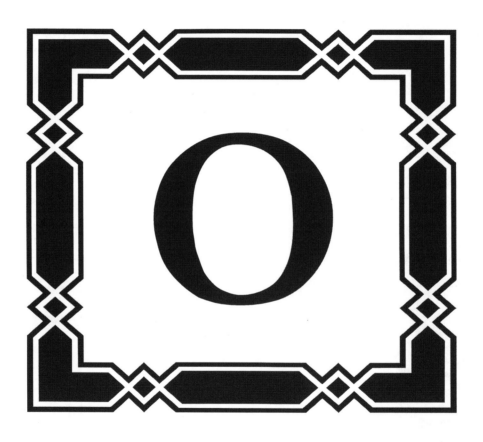

# You are...

O_____

# You are...

# P_____

# You are...

# Q

# You are...

# R_____

# You are...

## S_____

# You are...

T_____

You are...

U_____

You are...

V_____

You are...

W_____

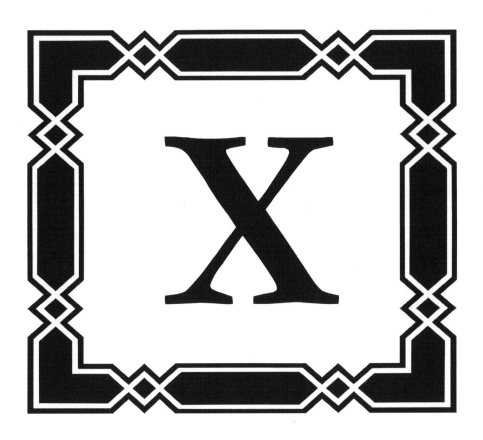

You are...

X_____

You are...

Y_____

You are...

Z_____

Thank You!

# Also In This Series

My Dad/Papa A to Z

My Mom/Mum/Mama A to Z

My Son A to Z

My Daughter A to Z

My Husband A to Z

My Wife A to Z

My Sister A to Z

My Brother A to Z

My Uncle A to Z

My Aunt/Auntie/Aunty A to Z

My Grandpa/Grandad/Gramps A to Z

My Grandma/Granny/Nanny/Gran/Nana/Nan A to Z

My Best Friend/Bestie A to Z

My Girlfriend A to Z

My Boyfriend A to Z

My Partner A to Z